I0162348

Exceptional Miracles in God's Glory
Supernatural journey of God's miracles

Written by Dana Satterfield

Scriptures verses are taken from the King James Version of the Bible unless otherwise noted.

Cover designed, rewritten and edited by:
Keeton's Self-Publishing & Consulting Services

Copyright © 2011 by Dana Satterfield

All rights reserved. No part of this book may be reproduced, stored in a retrieval system, or transmitted in any form or by any means. Not by electronic, mechanical, photocopy, recording, or any other without the prior permission of the publisher.

Printed in the United States of America

TABLE OF CONTENTS

Introduction

1. The Exception

2. Broke Foot

3. 90 Day Probation

4. Closed Account

5. No Food

6. The Accident

7. Maternity Leave

8. The Light Bill

9. No Check on Payday

10. Extended Leave

11. Court Date

Introduction

Exceptional miracles came about when I was first employed with a banking institute. Things began to unfold and unravel during my employment there as management was not upholding there promise for me becoming permanent after my probationary period was up.

God told me I was the exception to miracles happening in my life. Many people have to wonder if miracles really are true and if a miracle would ever happen to them. The bible tells us about miracle after miracle that Jesus performs. Unless you can see a miracle and experience a miracle doubt begin to cripple your mind. We are in a generation where they have to see it in order to believe it.

Miracles are really for the unbeliever. It's the unbeliever who needs to see miracles, signs and wonders in order for them to believe. Well I am here to tell you miracles are happening everyday to somebody on earth and I am one of them. Exceptional Miracles in God's Glory is basically self explanatory. You will see and experience miracle after miracle that actually happened to me.

The same God that performed these miracles in my life is the same God that will do the same for you if you just believe by faith. Faith is the things that you hope for and the evidence of the things that you don't see. You have to have faith in the unseen realm in order to believe in God's miracles to take place in your life.

I pray that your faith will be ignited so you too can begin to experience God's miracles in your life. Miracles can happen to anyone, anywhere at anytime. All you have to do is believe.

Dedication

O give thanks unto the Lord. Call upon His name; make known his deeds among the people. Psalms 105:1.

All glory and honor and praise to my Lord and Savior, Master Jesus Christ. He is my God of comfort and God of Support when I am in need, Jehovah-Jireh (My Provider). In the midst of my storm, Jehovah Shalom (My Peace). When sought for guidance, Jehovah Rohi (My Shepard). When I endured pain, Jehovah Rapha (My Healer).

You are worthy to be praised, Hallelujah! Thank you for developing my faith and trust through past adversities. I praise your name for spiritual and physical growth. Without You I wouldn't exist. Oh give thanks unto the Lord, for He is good, because His Mercy endureth forever. Psalms 118:1.

*I hold the key to my destiny and
that key is the word of God.*

Thanks

I would like to begin by saying thanks to my grandmother, Ms. Lillie Mae Wilson. She is the strongest, loving, supportive, and encouraging woman of God in my life. She has raised me with integrity, morals, and values. Thank You for your unceasing prayers over my life and the spiritual guidance that led me right to the cross. Thank you for imparting the word of God in my life at an early age. I love you, and I made it just like you said I would... Hallelujah!!!

Thanks to my children Rodney, Tania, and Byron whom are gifts from the Lord. They all have encouraged and prayed for me. Mama loves you with all my heart.

Thanks to my brother Timothy for your love, encouragement, and support. I love you baby brother.

And last but not least, thanks to my college instructor, Ms. Ruth Rector. You have taught me so much in and out of the classroom. Thank you for your support, prayers and having such a big heart for me and my children. I will always love you.

The power in prayer that changes any situation, all you have to do is believe and have faith.

The Exception

Chapter 1

The Exception

But without faith it is impossible to please him: for he that cometh to God must believe that he is, and that he is a rewarder of them that diligently seek him. Hebrews 11:6

I remembered in 1991 when I was 21 years old, just a young adult. I had a son who was 5 years old at the time. It was time for my yearly physical and I went in calmly as I normally do every year to get a complete physical. In the midst of the physical, the doctor advised me that there was a problem. I was told that I had an incompetent cervix which was abnormal in my case for my age. This meant if I decided to conceive more children, I wouldn't be unable to carry to the full term of 9 months. The doctor went on to say that I would have to abort early in the pregnancy stage. He felt it was best for me to get a hysterectomy right away at the age of 21. At this time, I had a delayed response thinking to myself, never able to bare more children at such a young age. What if I decided to get married and wanted to have more children with my husband. Suddenly fear grasps my heart and I asked the Lord God to help me with this decision. While waiting on an answer from the Lord, the doctor proceeded on to say that I had only one year to conceive then after that I couldn't have any more children.

I anxiously agreed to surgery out of fear without hearing a word from the Lord. The doctor left the room to prepare the paperwork for surgery. I laid on the side of the bed in fear and cried out to the Lord asking, "What do you want me to do?"

I saw a bright figure of an angel that descended on the side of my bed and held my hand. I clearly heard the Lord say, I created your womb to be fruitful and multiply.

The Lord said trust me not man. I heard the Lord say I didn't give you the spirit of fear but of power, love and of a sound mind (2Timothy 1:7). I discovered that God will give you peace in the midst of adversity. Hallelujah!!! Thank you Jesus, you are worthy to be praised.

Meanwhile, a spirit of peace fell upon me. The doctor returned back into the room with the surgery paperwork which had the appointment time on it. I advised the doctor that I had a change of heart about the surgery. He was in total rage as Satan would be. Satan came so close to stealing my womb, killing my spirit and destroying my seed.

I told the doctor that I will seek a second opinion. The doctor stated that where ever I decided to go, I will get the same diagnoses. I told him that the Lord is my second opinion. When the Lord advise me that I can no longer bare children then and only then will I accept this.

I left the doctors office and proceeded to bind and rebuke the spirit of death off of my womb. I walked out of there with victory giving the Lord Jesus Christ the glory. Hallelujah!!! 5 years later after the doctor diagnosis, the Lord blessed me to conceive my daughter, and 3 years after that a son. Amen. Thank you Jesus!!! God you are so merciful.

This is when I knew I was an exception in the Lord's eyes. Once again He manifested His glory in my situation. Praise Him!!!

I trust the Lord completely and stood still. I have seen his salvation prevail in me, my womb and my life. We walk by faith and not by sight. 2 Corinthians 5:7

What is your **"The Exception"** testimony that took place in your life or in someone else life that you know about?

_____

_____

_____

_____

_____

_____

_____

_____

_____

What is your **"The Exception"** testimony that took place in your life or in someone else life that you know about?

_____

_____

_____

_____

_____

_____

_____

_____

_____

What is your **"The Exception"** testimony that took place in your life or in someone else life that you know about?

_____

_____

_____

_____

_____

_____

_____

_____

Broken Foot

Chapter 2

Broken Foot

But I will restore you in health and heal your wounds declares the Lord. Jeremiah 30:17

It was one hot day in April 2004. I was tutoring after school and assisting with passing out the juice and crackers to the children. We had ran out of juice and my assistant went to get another case of juice. When she returned, the box slipped out of her hands and fell on my right foot. Keep in mind, I had on sandals at the time. I don't know what moved me more, the tears I seen in her eyes or the box that was accidently dropped on my right foot. She apologized for what happened. I told her I was fine while looking down on my right foot. It was so swollen that I had to pry my shoe off of my foot. I continued to work until the end of the day. I was thinking it is probably just a sprain and that I would go to the emergency room after work. Me and my daughter went to the emergency room and the doctor did just that. The doctor ran x-rays. The doctor came back with the results of my x-rays, and showed me where my foot was broken into 2 places on the top. This frightened me because I had never had anything broken on my body before. Of course, I started to cry. The doctor stated that I would have to be on crutches with my foot wrapped and will also have to wear a special shoe until I could be referred to a foot specialist in 2 days.

He looked at me and said he was going to prescribed me some medicine for pain. I told him I didn't feel anything. Then the doctor proceeds on to ask if I was numb. I told him no and that I was not in any pain. Next he said; well tell the person who drove you here, to meet you in the front. I told the doctor that I drove myself. He asked me how did I drive with a broke foot. I replied, I didn't know my foot was broke.

He then looked at me and shook his head and said who will be driving you home? Lastly I said I am driving myself home.

So after I was discharged, my daughter and I went home. I elevated my foot for 2 days. Meanwhile, people were calling and praying for me. Each morning I had to grab the crutches to walk. On the 3rd day I had to go the foot specialist in Town East Mall. They did a foot x-ray on my foot and confirmed a cast wouldn't correct the damage of my foot. The Specialist stated the bone was so damaged that he had to resort to surgery. Then said the surgery would be in 8 days. They scheduled an appointment for me to have surgery in 8 days.

When I left from their office and got in my car, I cried out to the Lord. Lord, I have never had anything broke on my body or surgery and I wasn't pleased with what the doctor said. I heard the Lord say, "Do you trust me?" I replied, "Completely". Then the Lord says, I will heal you.

After this I totally trust God. I got up one morning and heard the Lord say the next person that say they heard you broke your foot, tell them the doctor say my foot is broke but the Lord said I am healed. My mom called and said, I heard you broke your foot and are you alright? Do you need any medicine?

I explained to my mom, that he doctor said that my foot was broke but the Lord said I am healed. No response. She asked me if I was in pain and I told her no. She then said, how is your foot broke and you don't have any pain. I simply told her, the Lord said He is healing me.

Later on into the week I started walking without the crutches and begin telling the Lord every morning that I trust him on His word. Now it is Sunday morning and I am getting ready for church. The Lord tells me to take my right shoe. My children ask me why am I taking a shoe for my right foot and I can't even wear it. I told them the Lord told me to take it and that's that.

On my crutches, we arrived at church and the anointing of the Lord is so high that I heard the Lord say, "If you praise me I will heal you". *I heard Satan say you know if you praise the Lord on your broke foot you will break it in more places that you already have.* The Lord didn't give me a time to ponder on what Satan said. The Holy Ghost hit me and I started praising the Lord so much that everyone stopped praising the Lord and began watching me praise Him.

After I finished praising the Lord, I didn't have on any shoes or crutches holding me up. The pastor called me to the altar and said Sister Satterfield, are you ok? I replied I feel fine and walked back to my seat not realizing that I was walking without my crutches. The pastor stated that I was a true miracle and he has never seen a healing like the one the Lord just performed for me. I went to church on crutches and left healed and walking. Amen.

The next morning which was Monday I had an appointment to go to the foot specialist to prepare for surgery. In reality I was really going to see confirmation of my healing the Lord had just did on my foot.

17

When I arrived the Lord had the nurse to do an x-ray of the suppose-to-be broke foot. When she did, the foot specialist looked at the x-ray and said go get another x-ray because that is not her foot.

I went in the room and waited for the specialist and he walked through the door as if he seen a ghost. He looked at me and put both x-rays on the monitor before and after and asked me what happened to me over the week. I replied God happened. He said Ms. Satterfield when you came in here 8 days ago the bone on the top of your foot was broken into two places and now on this x-ray we just took, it shows your foot as if you have never broke it. He said, "I don't understand this, and in the 25 years that I have been in practice have never seen nothing like this before".

He told me my foot was no longer broken. I replied, I know it is not broken because the Lord told me if I praise him that he would heal me. I just came to get confirmation that the Lord healed me.

He looked at the nurse and told her there is nothing else for us to do for Ms. Satterfield her foot is no longer broken, she can be released to go back to work.

Hallelujah the Lord is good. I told him miracles signs and wonders are for the unbelievers.

What is your **"Broken Foot"** testimony that took place in your life or in someone else life that you know about?

_____

_____

_____

_____

_____

_____

_____

_____

_____

"Broken Foot" testimony that took place in your life or in someone else life that you know about?

_____

_____

_____

_____

_____

_____

_____

_____

_____

What is your **"Broken Foot"** testimony that took place in your life or in someone else life that you know about?

_____

_____

_____

_____

_____

_____

_____

_____

90-Day Probation

Chapter 3

90-Day Probation

Now faith is the substance of things hoped for, the evidence of things not seen. Hebrews 11:1

In 1997 I started working at this well-known bank as a teller. In the interview I was advised that I would start out as a part-time teller for 1 year with a raise at the end of my first year. After this I could work as a full-time teller. I agreed with the exception of me working full-time at the end of my first year.

I was told that if I need to take a day off, to give a 24-48 hours notice in order for them to make arrangements for my absence. Eleven months later I had an appointment and I gave my manger a 7 day notice ahead of time to prepare for my absence. Three days has passed since I gave my notice so I decided to remind my manager that I had an up and coming appointment. The day of my appointment I called into to work that morning to refresh my manager's memory on my absence and that I will be returning back to work the next day. Once I finished my appointment I requested documentation to justify for my absence. When I retuned to work the next day, I turned in my documentation and proceeded to work as usual.

This day was an exciting day for me because it is time for my evaluation and to receive a raise. Amen. I've noticed throughout the day my manager called each of my co-workers in one-by-one and finally she called me in. She advised me that I wasn't getting a raise and that I was on a 90 day probation due to my prior absence. I questioned the purpose of the 90 day probation when I followed the proper employment procedures. I reminded her that I gave her a 7 day notice, a 3 day notice, and then a day of notice for my absence. She stated that I didn't give her a notice for my absence and plus because she didn't speak with me.

This is considered a no call no show to work. I tell you, this took all the strength in my body to hold back my tears because I went above and beyond to make sure I covered my entire basis in advance. I heard the Holy Ghost whisper (*For we are taking pains to do what is right, not only in the eyes of the Lord but also in the eyes of men. 2Corinthians 8:21*). I then told her that she had my documentation confirming the day of my appointment. She said I would have to wait until my 90 day probation was up to be evaluated and to be considered for a raise. She then further stated that I had to remain as a part-time teller during the 90 day probation. My manager informed me that the personnel department implemented in the employee handbook that no one can be moved to another position with the company while on probation.

Right before we finished, she wanted me to sign papers stating that I didn't call in or give a notice of absence. Of course I refused to sign and walked off and went into the restroom. I fell on my knees and cried out to the Lord. I felt so hurt, I told the Lord God I did

24

nothing wrong and that I did everything right and in the end I was penalized. I said God you promised me a promotion and full-time employment. I was so angry with my manager that I asked the Lord to move her. I wanted to go over her head and report her but instead I heard the Lord said, "Avenge not yourselves, but rather give place unto wrath, for it is written, vengeance is mine". I will repay saith the Lord. Romans 12:19.

After the Lord spoke this to me, I felt a peace in my spirit. I wiped the tears cleaned from my face and went back to work. Seven days later everyone was called into a meeting. We were advised that one of our managers would be leaving. When I looked around I seen my manager standing and announcing she was the one leaving and stated that she didn't know why she just had to leave. Hallelujah!!!!! The Lord was moving on my behalf. She proceeded to say she will be working for another 7 days before being transferred to another bank.

Of course by this time, I left the meeting and went into the restroom to thank the Lord for moving on my behalf. The Lord told me he did this because I am the exception.

In the process of her leaving another manager from downtown came to replace her. My manager advised the new manager that I was on a 90 day probation and that I couldn't be moved or given a raise until after my 90 day probation was up. Prior to leaving, the assistant manager was aware that I was close to being with the company for a year and advised me to search the intranet for full time employment through the bank. She also mentioned she would give a great reference. I applied daily for positions throughout the bank. The new manager noticed I was applying for another position and told me I was wasting my time because I couldn't be moved due to being on a 90 day probation.

I heard the Lord say to me to tell her that I am the exception and the Lord would move me quickly. She laughed and replied in the 15 years she has worked for the company, she have never had a person to be moved while on probation. I advised her that the Lord will move me and she will see how quickly he moves.

What bothered me about her, she said the Lord just blessed her with a 150,000.00 home and her mortgage was only 700.00 a month. I said if the Lord blessed you with a 150,000 home with a low mortgage surely he can move me. She walked off.

Thereafter, the Lord advised me to anoint myself, my work space and start taking my things home daily to prepare the work station for the next teller. (Go thy way: and as thou hast believed, so be it done unto thee Matthew 8:14). I did this for the next 3 days then on the 5th day I was called in for an interview. I called in to speak with my manager that morning to advise her I will be a little late due to an early interview. She told me to go ahead with the interview but return to work afterwards.

After the interview I asked the Lord to confirm if I had the job. After arriving to work about 30 minutes later, I seen this young lady that I just seen downtown in the building where I had the interview. She was standing in my line to cash her check. There were other tellers to help her but she insisted on waiting for me. She stepped up and said the Lord told her to tell me that I had the job. I then praised the lord and she praised the Lord along with me. The Lord advised me that I would receive a call in 8 days. Eight days later a message was left on my desk when I returned from lunch. The note said for me to call personnel. Of course Satan tried to convince me that the call was just to notify me that I couldn't be moved. As always, I commanded Satan to get thee behind me in Jesus name.

I called personnel and spoke with the recruiter that advised me that I was considered for the job I applied for. She had to speak with my manager to see if I could be released. I praised the Lord so loud that everyone in the bank stopped and looked at me. I gave the Lord the glory and magnified him before all men. Still Satan came back to say you won't get the job once personnel find out you are on a 90 day probation. I bind and rebuked Satan and any negative thoughts that tried to rest upon my mind.

Later that day the assistant manager came up to me and said personnel had contacted her and she had some good news and some bad news. I asked for the bad news first. She said I couldn't be moved. Then I asked what was the good news? She said I couldn't be moved for 2 weeks and asked if this was alright. I had to stay for another 2 weeks in order to give them time to replace me. Hallelujah!!!! She praised the Lord with me then the new manager came over and stated once personnel find out I was on a 90 day probation they would not allow me to be moved. I told her I serve a big God and if the Lord is for me who can be against me. She looked at me and took 2 steps back and then I proceeded to tell her the Lord is going to bless me because I am the exception in Jesus name to every man-made rule.

Upon leaving, the new manager called personnel to see why I was being moved with a 90 probation status. Personnel then told her that they don't see where I was on probation of any kind. I went to personnel to sign paperwork to be transferred downtown and because I wasn't given a raise the Lord gave me double for my trouble. He blessed me with 2 raises. One for being transferred and the other one for the raise I was in titled to before my original manager left.

Hallelujah!!!! Lord you are worthy to be praised.

What is your **"90-Day Probation"** testimony that took place in your life or in someone else life that you know about?

_____

_____

_____

_____

_____

_____

_____

_____

_____

What is your **"90-Day Probation"** testimony that took place in your life or in someone else life that you know about?

_____

_____

_____

_____

_____

_____

_____

_____

What is your **"90-Day Probation"** testimony that took place in your life or in someone else life that you know about?

_____

_____

_____

_____

_____

_____

_____

_____

Closed Account

Chapter 4

Closed Account

Thou art the God that doest wonders; thou hast declared thou
strength among the people.
Psalms 77:14

I have read in Mark, Matthew, Luke, and John the
miraculous miracles Jesus performed. I have seen how He
performed these miracles in my life. Sometimes we tend
to forget how wonderful God is in his Glory. He brought
back to my remembrance the year I was employed with a
major banking institute in Dallas, Texas. I worked there
for many years.

I purchased a truck and paid monthly payments of $480.
By the way, this truck is a great significance to my story.
On payday I set aside my tithes and offering. I then
focused on paying the bills. Once I finished paying all of
the bills, I only had my truck note left to pay. *You know
how that goes; your money is gone before you even get paid.* I
thought to myself, if I pay my truck note, I will not have
any money to get back and forth to work. So, what did I
do? I am glad you asked.

I prayed and call forth a financial increase. I asked the
Lord to perform a sudden financial miracle in my finances
and the Lord did just that. The bibles states in Matthew
7:7; ask and it shall be given to you. I give all the glory
and the praise to God. He is truly worthy to be praised
and magnified.

Well 30 days earlier, I closed my checking account and opened up a new one with a Credit Union.

I started to throw away my old debit card to the old bank but the Lord told me to keep the inactive debit card. I obeyed the Lord and put the card back in my purse.

It is Friday and I am on my way to church. First I decided to get a money order for my truck note then I will drop it off after church. There was a change in plans when I got to church. The pastor was speaking on faith which is my favorite subject. He went on to say that the Lord revealed to him that who ever would step out on faith and gives a sacrificial offering would receive a double portion for their troubles within 24 hours. This excited me because you can't out give God. I sat there seeing that all I had was $480 (truck note) to my name. So I said Lord I need double for my troubles and I believe that you will bless me but all I have is $480.

I asked the Lord how much do you want me to give, and the Lord said $480. I said Lord that is all I have and He said, "that is all I want". So of course, I thought to myself I need confirmation on this. Then I said to myself, the Lord didn't say that. I went to my pastor and asked what should I give as a sacrificial offering. The pastor looked at me and said give whatever the Lord told you to give. So that answered that question. I filled out the offering envelope and sowed the $480 by faith. I gave this in faith and believing that would get my double blessing as God promised within 24 hours. Amen.

My son asked me after church, mama your truck note is due tomorrow what are you going to do? I looked at him and said wait on the Lord then we went home. I went to sleep and the next morning I woke up to a still small voice in my ears telling me to get up and go to the ATM machine.

I said, Lord I don't have anything in my checking account. The Lord spoke again, daughter get up and go to the ATM machine.

I got up; put my clothes and shoes on then went into my oldest son room to let him know where I was going. He said but you don't have any money in the bank. I went to the ATM Machine down the street from my house. I reached for my ATM bank card as the Lord instructed me to do. I heard the Lord say, "Not that one". I thought I only have one active bank card. The Lord said take the inactive bank card to make a withdraw. Of course now fear tried to grasp my heart because I am trying to figure out what the Lord has already worked out. I heard Satan say you know that card is not any good and if you put that card in there the machine will not give it back. I didn't ponder on this because the Lord has never failed me.

I put the card into the ATM and entered my 4-digit code and pressed balance inquiry. I stood there and looked at the ATM machine like I have seen a ghost. The balance showed $960. I screamed GLORY! GLORY! GLORY! HALLELUJAH!!!! I started praising the Lord in front of the ATM machine and in front of everyone that passed by rather car, truck, or just walking.

I cried and bent over and said Lord you are so worthy. After I came to myself I thought I first have to get a receipt because no one will believe I withdrew money from a closed account. Once the receipt had printed then Satan said, that is an error and you don't have any money in a closed account. Always remember when the Lord is about to bless you, Satan is in the midst to discourage you and try to make you doubt what the Lord has promised you. Amen.

I went on ahead and pressed withdraw and the entire amount of $960 came out. I heard the Lord say; because you trusted me I will continue to bless you. He told me to tell others about the miracle he had just performed before my eyes. I had to sit in the truck for about 5-10 minutes to get a grip on what the Lord had just done for me. I then went home, called my pastor and told him the miraculous news.

He praised the Lord with me then got very quiet when I told him the withdrawal was out of a closed account. All he could say was, my Lord, my Lord. You know the Lord is so awesome that it is scary sometimes.

I knew then how the Lord felt in Deuteronomy when the children of Israel had doubt after all the miracles the Lord performed before them. I went a step further and called the bank on the following Monday morning to confirm my checking account was closed. I spoke to the lady by the name of Diane and she stated that my account had been closed for 30 days and there was no way a deposit or withdraw could have been processed. I just held the phone for a moment and thanked Diane for confirmation and continued to praise the Lord.

I have learned to walk by faith. Now faith is the substance of things hoped for the evidence of things not seen. Hebrews 11:1.

What is your **"Closed Account"** testimony that took place in your life or in someone else life that you know about?

_____

_____

_____

_____

_____

_____

_____

_____

_____

What is your **"Closed Account"** testimony that took place in your life or in someone else life that you know about?

_____

_____

_____

_____

_____

_____

_____

_____

_____

What is your **"Closed Account"** testimony that took place in your life or in someone else life that you know about?

_____

_____

_____

_____

_____

_____

_____

_____

_____

No Food

Chapter 5

No Food

I have been young, and now am old; yet have I never
seen the righteous forsaken, nor his seed begging bread.
Psalms 37:25

I was working part-time and receiving government
assistance for food at this stage in my life. I had an
appointment for recertification on a day I was required
to work. If you have ever been on government
assistance, when your appointment is scheduled it is
very vital that you are on time. For any reason if you
miss your appointment you would have to wait another
month for assistance. Because of work, I didn't make
my appointment. I prayed to the Lord and then called
my caseworker to see if she would allow me to walk-in
for immediate assistance. She advised me to come but
stated that she can't guarantee that I would receive help
for the current month I'm seeking help for but on the
other hand I would receive help for the following
month.

I was persistent due to the fact that it was the week of
Thanksgiving and my children and I had no food in the
refrigerator or cabinets. I finally got to meet with my
caseworker that told me by it being close to the end of
the month already, I would have to wait until the 2nd
week of December to receive funds for food.
I was happy that I still qualified for assistance.

I said, "Lord what will my children eat"? Here I was in a bad situation but then I looked at God and not my situation. I said, "Ok Lord, I trust You on this one". I told the Lord my desire was to cook a big dinner for Thanksgiving.

The Lord led me to a powerful scripture; Isaiah 40:31 and it reads: but they that wait upon the Lord shall renew their strength; they shall mount up with wings as eagles; they shall run and not be weary, they shall walk and not faint. Amen!

I arrived to my home and I heard Satan say, call your mom or your best friend and tell them you don't have any food for yourself nor your children. Satan also said if you don't call, you will not have anything to eat. I immediately heard the Lord say be still and know that I am the Lord your God. God then told me to go into the kitchen and anoint every cabinet and my refrigerator and decree an overflow of food to come forth. I obeyed the Lord and did just what he asked me to do. I stopped look at what I didn't have and start believing in what the Lord was about to do for us.

At this time I started praising the Lord for filling all the cabinets, refrigerator and freezer full of food. For the word says God shall supply all of my needs according to Philippians 4:19. After praising and worshipping the Lord for his goodness I heard the Lord say commit thy way unto him trust also in him and he shall bring it to past; Psalms 37:5. Hallelujah!!!! To the Glorious name of my Lord and Savior, I then felt an unspeakable peace come over me.

I prayed and went to sleep. Around 12 midnight, I woke up to the voice of the Lord instructing me to call and check the account balance on my food card. Here it is Thanksgiving morning and I spoke to God and told Him it was going to be December 15th until I receive the deposit on my food card.

I heard the Lord say call and check your food account balance. I obeyed the Lord and called. I waited to hear the balance on the automatic recorder and it stated that I had an available balance of $960.00.

HALLELUJAH!!! Not only did God show up but He also showed out. He gave me double for my troubles.

I praised the Lord on bended knees with tears flowing down my face on Thanksgiving Day! I was able to cook dinner for my children as well as sow food into other family lives that were less fortunate.

Please note: My monthly food account balance is $435.00. So I thought that the $960.00 was for the end of November and also for the month of December. In December the Lord blessed me with the regular monthly balance of $435 as well.

Glory be to the Lord of God for His mercy and grace is sufficient. God is worthy to be praised.

What is your **"No Food"** testimony that took place in your life or in someone else life that you know about?

_____

_____

_____

_____

_____

_____

_____

_____

What is your **"No Food"** testimony that took place in your life or in someone else life that you know about?

_____

_____

_____

_____

_____

_____

_____

_____

What is your **"No Food"** testimony that took place in your life or in someone else life that you know about?

_____

_____

_____

_____

_____

_____

_____

_____

_____

The Accident

Chapter 6

The Accident

Thou shalt obey the voice of the Lord thy God, and do his
commandments and his statues, which I command thee this
day. Deuteronomy 27:10

All this week I was attending a church revival. At this
time, I was given a prophesy to start anointing my body
from head to toe with anointing oil every morning. The
next morning I was in such a hurry to get to work that I
forgot to anoint my entire body but I did anoint my
head. I got in the car turned on Yolanda Adam's cd and
drove on to work. Half way to my job the Holy Spirit
told me to turn back around and anoint myself with oil
from head to toe. I looked at the clock in my car and
said Lord I am 10 minutes away from work, I can't be
late to work. I then proceeded to turn the music up
higher and heard the Lord say again, turn around now,
go back home and anoint yourself with oil. So I prayed
that the Lord would give me favor with my manager
whom I called to explain that I was 5 minutes away
from work and had left something very important at
home. I told him I needed to go back and retrieve it.
He stated that I could go and he wouldn't hold this
against me.

I turned the car around and went home to anoint myself
with oil from head to toe. After doing so, I felt light as

if I was having an outer body experience. I went on ahead back to work. Later that afternoon me and a female co-worker went to lunch whom I would daily talk to about Jesus.

On this particular day she was the one talking to me about the Lord and was thanking me for ministering to her and wanted to know more about the Lord.

I would never forget this day because all day long I felt very strange as if something was about to happen but I couldn't figure it out. It was the end of the workday which was Friday and payday today. I left the building telling everyone I would see them later since we had weekends off. I got on the elevator and got off on the ground floor (1st floor). I proceeded to exit the building at this time.

Important Note of this story: The female co-worker that I had lunch with earlier said the Lord had instructed her to go after me before I left the building because I was in danger, but she stated that she couldn't get any of the elevators to open to catch up with me in time. So she ran down 5 flights of stares to try and stop me from exiting the building. She said once she made it to the ground floor (1st floor), she saw me step off the curve then walk across the street. She was watching me through the glass while still inside the building. She started running toward the door yelling out my name. She yelled my name twice but when she got to the door what had came of out her mouth was JESUS! She said after she yelled JESUS! She seen me in the street and two tall angels as tall as telephone poles swooped down on each side of me and then it happened.......the accident occurred.

I felt a hit but didn't know what had hit me. I was in the middle of the street dazed, dismayed and bent over wandering what had just happened. Psalms 91:11 says; for he shall give his angels charge over thee, to keep thee in al thy ways.

I heard my co-worker call my name and assisted me from the street to the curb where I sat down.

She said she will call the police and the ambulance. I am still wandering what just happened and why am I so dazed. The ambulance came and spoke with my co-worker and asked her where the person in the accident was. I heard her say; there she is sitting on the curb. The paramedics came over to assist me. They began to ask questions such as what year is it? What is my name? Who is the president? Do I know where I am? I had answered all the questions correctly. They asked if I wanted to go to the hospital for observation, I said I would drive myself there. The paramedics said, "We didn't come out here for nothing, we are taking somebody to the hospital". I laughed and said alright I'll go. As I was climbing into the ambulance, one of the paramedics said don't climb in, you are going in style. He pulled out the stretcher and advised me to lie down.

I was taken to Methodist Hospital for observation. The doctor ran 3 consecutive tests on me which they were all negative. I was told to lie in my room until I was released. While I was lying there I over heard people in the hall talking about the accident on Elm Street. It didn't dawn on me that I was the one that they were referring to until the police officer came into my room. The police officer asked me my name, who was the president and the date? He also asked me if I knew where I was. Again, I answered all of the questions correctly. He had a police report in his hand and asked if I knew why I was here. I said no I don't.

The police officer said, Miss you don't know what happened? I said no I don't. He said, would you like for me to tell you why you are here. I replied, yes please. The policeman stated that I was in a very bad accident and that I got hit by a truck (1500). I looked at him with amazement and speechless.

He said the truck was going about 45mph and my mouth dropped. The policeman asked me how far was I thrown. I explained to him that I wasn't.
He then asked me if I had broken anything in my body. I told him no.

He asked well, what was sprained, any swollen joints or soreness. I told him nothing, I am fine but I did request 2 aspirins due to the slight headache I had.

He looked at me as if he had seen a ghost and left out looking at the report. The other office came back in and said Miss you are a miracle, the Lord saved you. I have never seen nothing like it. I just want to tell you that the Lord is good. Oh give thanks unto the Lord; He is good, because his mercy endures forever. Psalms 118:1. Amen.

What is your **"The Accident"** testimony that took place in your life or in someone else life that you know about?

_____

_____

_____

_____

_____

_____

_____

_____

What is your **"The Accident"** testimony that took place in your life or in someone else life that you know about?

_____

_____

_____

_____

_____

_____

_____

_____

What is your **"The Accident"** testimony that took place in your life or in someone else life that you know about?

_____

_____

_____

_____

_____

_____

_____

_____

Maternity Leave

Chapter 7

Maternity Leave

Be still and know that I am God, I will be exalted among the
nations and I will be exalted in the earth. Psalms 46:10

March of 1999, I had to go on a paternity leave due to
the high risk pregnancy I had. Normally in the 3rd
month of my pregnancies a one day surgery would
have to be performed to insure my cervix wouldn't
open too early during the stage of my pregnancy. This
was to prevent bed rest for the entire pregnancy and
from going into early labor.

When I made it to the 4th month of the pregnancy, I was
told by my doctor that my child wouldn't have a chance
to live and suggested that I abort to avoid
disappointment. Well of course fear tried to grasp my
heart. He mentioned that there was nothing else he
could do. No use of holding onto a child that didn't
stand a chance was his exact words. I began quoting
scriptures. In 2 Timothy 1:7 it reads; The Lord does not
give us a spirit of fear but of power, love and a sound
mind. I told the doctor I will not allow anyone or
anything take to what the Lord has blessed me with. I
know that every good gift and every perfect gift is from
above, and cometh down from the Father of lights, with
whom is no variableness neither shadows of turning.
This is quoted from James 1:7.

I went on to tell the doctor that I believe in God, Jesus Christ and I declare I will have my child in Jesus name. He shall live and not die.

I started binding and rebuking death and all of Satan assignments against me and my womb. I requested another doctor. Three months later I went into labor. The labor was delayed because it appeared my son lungs collapsed and I had to get steroid shots injected into my hips for 2 days. The doctor was still telling me that my child might not make it. I confessed and professed life over my child until my child was born. For the rest of his life he shall live and not die.

I waited for the Lord to prevail in my situation and in 2 days God showed up and showed out.

HALLELUJAH!!! A 2lbs. 1oz child was born and was given an APGAR test. This test is given to infants to determine their mobility skills. My son passed the test with flying colors. What amazed the doctors was the strength that my son had and yet so small. He was the size of an aerosol can at the same time; he was courageous and very strong. The doctor that delivered him came in and stated he has never seen a baby that small with so much fight in him. The doctor also went on to say, my son was so alert and active. He knows that the Lord saved him and has His hand on him. The doctor said he passed the test that full term babies normally failed.

The Lord is good and his mercy endures forever. The doctor even gave God the glory. Because of my sons low birth weight, he had to remain in the hospital for another 4 months. On the 5th month, he was released to go home. He was as healthy as a full term infant.

In everything I give thanks, for this is the will of God in Christ Jesus concerning you; 1 Thessalonians 5:18. By the way, my son name is Byron L. Tatum, II who is now 11 years old at the time of writing this book. Amen.

What is your **"Maternity Leave"** testimony that took place in your life or in someone else life that you know about?

_____

_____

_____

_____

_____

_____

_____

_____

What is your **"Maternity Leave"** testimony that took place in your life or in someone else life that you know about?

_____

_____

_____

_____

_____

_____

_____

_____

What is your **"Maternity Leave"** testimony that took place in your life or in someone else life that you know about?

_____

_____

_____

_____

_____

_____

_____

_____

Light Bill

Chapter 8

Light Bill

For thou, Lord will bless the righteous; with favor will thou
compass him as with a shield. Psalms 5:12

I remember looking for a place for my children and I to
live. The Lord led me to this 3 bedroom duplex. The
landlord that I met that day said it was a $700 deposit
required to move in. This was all I had at the time and I
thought to myself, how am I going to get my lights cut
on? I heard the Lord say in Proverbs 3:5-6; Trust in thy
Lord with all thou heart, lean not unto thou own
understanding but in all thou ways acknowledge him
and he shall direct my path.

I told the Lord that I trust him on this. I went to the
landlord and told him that I had the $700 deposit but
didn't have the money to get the lights cut on in my
name. I asked him if I could pay half of the deposit and
give him the other half in 2 weeks once I got paid. This
way I could use the other half to get the lights cut on.
He said he would take the $700 deposit and would keep
the lights on in his name until I got paid.

I tell you, the Lord is so good to me. We moved into
our new place. Two weeks later I called the landlord to
let him know that I just got paid and would be making
a deposit to get the lights cut on in my name. He

65

replied, Ms. Satterfield don't bother doing that right now, just keep them on in my name and focus on you and your children and their needs.

He said he would continue to keep the lights in his name for the next few months.

I dropped the phone and started praising the Lord like never before.

The Lord had my landlord to pay the lights in our house for 3 months.

Glory! Glory! Glory! Favor isn't fair but somebody got to have it. It might as well be me...

What is your **"The Light Bill"** testimony that took place in your life or in someone else life that you know about?

_____

_____

_____

_____

_____

_____

_____

_____

What is your **"The Light Bill"** testimony that took place in your life or in someone else life that you know about?

_____

_____

_____

_____

_____

_____

_____

_____

What is your **"The Light Bill"** testimony that took place in your life or in someone else life that you know about?

_____

_____

_____

_____

_____

_____

_____

_____

No Check on Payday

Chapter 9

No Check on Payday

But my God shall supply all your need according to his riches in glory by Christ Jesus. Philippians 4:19

I had started a new job where the manager had hired me on the spot. Meanwhile, I had to take a variety of tests and interview with the manager that hired me. There were a total of 21 people in my training class. We were all told that we will have to wait for about 3 weeks before we receive our first pay check. Everyone was complaining except for me about their bills and they couldn't wait that long for a paycheck. Others were stating how their utilities might get cut off and how they didn't have food to stretch that long.

I prayed to the Lord and asked for a miracle to take place in their lives. I asked the Lord for their paychecks to be released in 2 weeks instead of 3 weeks. After I prayed, I told the group that the Lord said he would bless them with their check in 2 weeks. *Key note: I said their checks.* They began to laugh and mock me, telling me I didn't know what I was talking about. I stood up at this time and said, "Is there anyone who would like to touch and agree with me that the Lord will provide the checks in 2 weeks?" Only 2 ladies stood up agreeing and believing. I called it done in Jesus Name.

I told the group that the Lord said he would bless them in the beginning of the 3rd week. They began to laugh again and said they will believe it when they see it.

 I started thanking the Lord for what he was about to do in our classroom.

There were 3 ladies sitting next to me telling me how they believe the Lord will provide. I told them it was a done deal and the Lord will establish this for us so everyone will see he is God.

Here it was the beginning of the 3rd week and our trainer walks in with white envelopes. Everyone looked as if they have seen a ghost. The Holy Ghost told me my trainer has everyone else check but mine. The trainer stood there and said she had an announcement to make. She had good news and bad news. I interjected, and stood up to say, you have everyone's check accept mine. She replied, yes Dana that is correct. How did you know I didn't have your check? I just smiled and sat down.

It was to my surprise how everyone was not happy about me not receiving my check, although they were happy to receive their paychecks. They told the trainer that if it wasn't for her prayers, they wouldn't have their checks. The group stated that they would go to Human Resources to demand my check and how it wasn't fair that I didn't receive one. They acknowledged how they laughed at me and still the Lord came through for them because of my prayers. The trainer explained how she never experienced not receiving only one person paycheck out of a group before. She began to apologize. I said praise the Lord, he has other plans for me.

The young lady that was sitting next to me asked what was I going to do. I told her I am going to trust in the Lord because he will provide for me. She advised me to go to the Human Resources Department to see if a check could be processed for me (*an off cycled check*). I didn't feel led to go so I didn't.

She said Ms. Dana if it wasn't for your prayers we wouldn't have received our checks. She offered her entire check to me so I could pay all my bills but I did not accept it. I told her I trust the Lord.

Hallelujah!! Praise the Lord. I was led to speak many blessings over her since she had an enormous heart for me and my children.

The trainer was moved by my positive reaction of not receiving a pay check that she went to the manager that hired me. She told him to go to Human Resources on my behalf and a get a check for me. Well he pulled me out of the class and we walked to the Human Resources office.
He stated that he has never heard of a training class missing one person's paycheck. Usually half of a training group would receive a check and the other would have to wait until the following week, but this was an unusual situation.

The manager asked me to wait outside while he go and speak to the payroll department. He came back with his head held low. I asked what was wrong.

They told him I would have to wait another week to receive my paycheck. I just smiled and said ok. He said, "Don't you have bills to pay?" I do. As a matter of fact, all of my bills are due. He asked, "What are you going to do?" I told him, I will wait on the Lord; he didn't bring me this far to leave me. The manager just looked at me and shook his head.

He then pulled me to the side and said, the company policy states managers or employees are not to accept gifts. This would be grounds for termination. He said he will write a personal check for the entire amount that my check would of have been. Before I could say something, he interjected and said, "I know you love the Lord and pray a lot so I know you have to pray about it first then get back to me". I began to laugh and said yes that is true. My manager said when the Lord gives you an answer; let me know the amount you need to pay all your bills and also enough food for you and your children and then I will write the check.

I went back into the classroom and to my surprise the entire class had gathered up money to give to me. The class mentioned how it was through their unbelief; they received a paycheck and not me. I told them that miracles, signs and wonders are for the unbelievers. When I got home from work, I prayed unto the Lord and asked him to confirm to me if this was him working through my manager. He confirmed that the He, the Lord is working through my manager to bless me.

Before I could even go to my manager at work, he had sent someone to get me so I could meet him at his desk. He asked me, "What did the Lord say?" I told him I accept the blessing and then he took out a piece of paper wrote these word; "How much do you need?" and slid the paper over to me. I wrote down $900 and he looked at me and said is this all? I told him yes.

He said he would have the check ready for me before I leave from work that day. Hallelujah!!!

Praise His holy name. This man didn't know me but he knew the spirit of the Lord that dwells in me. Amen.

What is your "No Check on Payday" testimony that took place in your life or in someone else life that you know about?

_____

_____

_____

_____

_____

_____

_____

_____

What is your **"No Check on Payday"** testimony that took place in your life or in someone else life that you know about?

_____

_____

_____

_____

_____

_____

_____

_____

What is your "No Check on Payday" testimony that took place in your life or in someone else life that you know about?

_____

_____

_____

_____

_____

_____

_____

_____

Extended Leave

Chapter 10

Extended Leave

A good man showed favor and landed' he will guide his
affairs with discretion. Psalms 112:5

I took 6 months leave because I was guaranteed
compensation due an accident I was in. I needed this
time off in order to recuperate from the accident. This
was truly a break and a blessing for me, not because of
the accident but because I had church revival every
night. For this reason, this would allow me to be in the
presence of the Lord more. Being away from work so
long I got to the point I didn't desire to have a secular
job anymore. I just wanted more of Jesus.

After I prayed, my manager called and advised me that
my 6 months leave was about to expire. He went on to
say if I choose to stay on my leave, it would have to be
without pay. I told him I wasn't ready to come back
and wanted to extend my leave for another 6 months.
He said he understood and hung the phone up.

I prayed to the Lord; I said God, man said my time has
expired and will not be compensated for the duration of
my extended leave. Your word said that You will give
me the desires of my heart so I delight myself in you.
God your word said ask and it shall be given unto me.
My 6 months has expired and I am trusting on the Lord
to sustain me…but God….but God…   Hallelujah!!
You are worthy.

After I received my last pay, I paid my tithes and offering, all the bills then I sowed a seed believing God will supply all of my needs for the next 6 months. Two weeks later the Holy Ghost whispered in my ear and told me to call and check the balance in your account. Now remember I am on another extended leave for 6 months without pay. This is what my manager told me.

I checked my account and heard the automotive service announce my account balance over the phone. I hollered, Lord your mercy and grace, I thank you Lord, you are worthy to be praised!" The balance that was in my account was the exact same amount I had in the previous months. For a moment I was puzzled. I called my manager and asked if my time had expired and he replied, yes. I told him I received a deposit in my checking account and he said he had turned in my time as he was instructed by his manager whom told him to sign off on my timesheet every two weeks. My manager said he didn't ask any questions, he was only following orders from what he was told to do.

This of course left me speechless. I did not doubt the Lord, it's when he blesses me, and he does it in a big way. He always gives me the desire of my heart and more… This really over took me; I had to call my managers' boss whom answered the phone. I explained to him what had happened and that I received another check into my account. I asked him have he submitted paperwork to personnel to stop payment on the check. He replied, "No Dana, as a matter of fact, I have your folder on my desk. He asked how I was doing. I replied I am blessed. He then went on to say; well you continue to rest and don't worry about the paperwork.

He said he will leave my folder on his desk for the next 6 months and I will be compensated. He then said, have a nice day and if I needed additional time off to call him. God opened doors that no man could close. God gave me favor beyond favor. Hallelujah! Jesus is worthy to be praised. I magnify and gratify my Lord and Savior. Amen.

What is your **"Extended Leave"** testimony that took place in your life or in someone else life that you know about?

_____

_____

_____

_____

_____

_____

_____

_____

_____

What is your **"Extended Leave"** testimony that took place in your life or in someone else life that you know about?

_____

_____

_____

_____

_____

_____

_____

_____

_____

What is your **"Extended Leave"** testimony that took place in your life or in someone else life that you know about?

_____

_____

_____

_____

_____

_____

_____

_____

Court Date

Chapter 11

Court Date

Thou wilt keep him in perfect peace, whose mind is stayed
on thee; because he trusted in thee. Isaiah 26:3

In 2007 I was on leave due to back problems. I was
going back and forth to the doctor for treatments.
Taking pain medicines was part of my life due to the
pain.

I was advised within 3 months of my leave that my job
decided to stop paying me due to the lack of
information the insurance company did not receive.
My doctor and I had already sent in all the information
that was requested prior to this. In the meantime,
everything fell behind on all of my financial
commitments.

This made it very hard for me to get accurate treatment
even though I had insurance. Whenever I had a doctor's
visit they required a co-pay for which I couldn't afford.
Things started spiraling down hill in my finances. My
new car had to go back, I didn't have any food and to
top it off the previous co-pastor I had trusted and
respected had lost her spouse. Due to this she suffered
mentally and had a relapse thinking my children were
her children and tried to take them from me.   I had
$5000 worth of furniture in the storage and it was sold

due to non-payment. I had a "Job" moment from the bible....but God Hallelujah!

I praised my way to victory and seeing "Job" situation in the bible is the same tool I used to break out of my adversity. I had a prayer partner that stuck with me through it and reminded me of who God is and has done in my life.

Due to my faith in God, I asked the Lord to forgive her for she knows not what she is doing and to deliver her and set her free. The word states to bless those who persecute you. I began to praise Him for this even in the midst of the trial. I was so focused on the Lord because I knew this was a temporary situation. I began praying to the Lord telling Him how great and mighty he is and how nothing is impossible with him on my side. So I filed an appeal which took 45 days to get a response.

Hallelujah! Praise the Lord! I am saying this because there is a God that sits high and look low. His word states he shall supply all of my needs according to his riches in glory by Christ Jesus.

I received a visit from the apartment manager where I resided. She stated that if I don't pay the past due rent of 2 months within 3 days; she was going to sit all of my furniture outside. In spite of it all, I felt a peace come over me. I told her while she stood there, that I filed an appeal and I haven't received a response yet. She said, "What are you going to do?" I looked at her and said I have done all that I could do; now the only thing to do is to wait on God. The apartment manager stepped back and looked at me as if she had seen a ghost. I told her that if I didn't have the money in 3 days, my children and I would leave graciously but please not to sit my furniture outside. I also told her she could just keep the furniture as payment.

She looked at me in amazement as if she couldn't believe what she was hearing. I told her that I would let her know once the Lord let me know, she said ok. Before she walked off, I told her to have a blessed day and she said ok then walked off. After the apartment manager left, I praised the Lord and cried out to him. I told him I have done all that I could do and I am casting all of my cares on him because he cares for me. Well 45 days later, I was denied again but I was at peace. I trust and knew the Lord would come through for me.

The assistant manager of the apartments told me that I will be served papers to go to court but not to worry and let this bother me because they were willing to work with me later.

I was served by a constable to appear in court. I still praised the Lord in the midst of adversity. The glory goes to God, not Satan.

You see, at times when we are faced with an adversity beyond our control we tend to fall into depression and forget that God still rules and reigns. We get so caught up in our problems that we forget we have a Problem Solver. We think if we are in an impossible situation, that it is impossible for the Lord to deliver us.

Well I am here to tell you that the devil is a lie and he has been defeated today, yesterday and forever more. I found out if the situation is too big for you; it is the perfect size for God, Amen and Amen.

I appeared in court where I met the assistant manager. She advised me again not to worry about anything and that we were just going to go through the proper procedures and motions. She said they would assist me and my children. This was confirmation from the Lord for what he had already revealed to me. The assistant manager of the apartments was saved and she loved the Lord just as I did. Amen.

There were people in the court room for the same reasons that I was there unable to pay rent and was there to plead their case, just like me. The assistant manger and I began to pray for the people. Hallelujah, I felt like "Job" in the bible. I stop focusing on my circumstances and started praying for others who were in the same predicament.

Once we were called up before the judge, I notice even the judge was as humble and saved as the assistant manager which the Lord sent to bless me.

I offered to work for the apartment complex for free to maintain my stay in the apartments. The judge said he had not heard of such an offer before and would leave that up the apartment complex.

While still living there, the Lord led me to an organization and gave me favor with management of that organization. Hallelujah!

This organization only provides assistants to those who are disabled. Hallelujah, God is awesome, omnipresent and omniscient. I called this organization and the lady that answered the phone told me the qualifications to receive assistance I didn't have all of what was required of me. The Lord told me to make the appointment anyway by faith and go. The Lord said he was going to open doors for me.

I went and the Lord truly blessed me. This organization paid *all* of my bills for 4 months. At this time I was still without compensation from my job. Hallelujah, glory be to God.

The apartment assistant manager that the Lord put in my pathway, I believed God used her to be a comfort to me in the midst of my adversity. I constantly spoke blessings in her life. She is truly sent from heaven and I thank the Lord for her daily.

At the end, I heard the Lord say, "Well done daughter you passed your test". Hallelujah!!

What is your **"Court Date"** testimony that took place in your life or in someone else life that you know about?

_____

_____

_____

_____

_____

_____

_____

_____

What is your **"Court Date"** testimony that took place in your life or in someone else life that you know about?

_____

_____

_____

_____

_____

_____

_____

_____

What is your **"Court Date"** testimony that took place in your life or in someone else life that you know about?

_____

_____

_____

_____

_____

_____

_____

_____

_____

Can you think of any miracles that happened to you or to someone else and you know without a doubt it had to be God?

_____

_____

_____

_____

_____

_____

_____

_____

Can you think of any miracles that happened to you or to someone else and you know without a doubt it had to be God?

_____

_____

_____

_____

_____

_____

_____

_____

Can you think of any miracles that happened to you or to someone else and you know without a doubt it had to be God?

_____

_____

_____

_____

_____

_____

_____

_____

Can you think of any miracles that happened to you or to someone else and you know without a doubt it had to be God?

_____

_____

_____

_____

_____

_____

_____

_____

If you don't have any miracles or testimonies to share, I pray God will do the impossible for you so you can share with others. Now you can write your own miracle.

_____

_____

_____

_____

_____

_____

_____

_____

If you don't have any miracles or testimonies to share, I pray God will do the impossible for you so you can share with others. Now you can write your own miracle.

If you don't have any miracles or testimonies to share, I pray God will do the impossible for you so you can share with others. Now you can write your own miracle.

_____

_____

_____

_____

_____

_____

_____

_____

If you don't have any miracles or testimonies to share, I pray God will do the impossible for you so you can share with others. Now you can write your own miracle.

_____

_____

_____

_____

_____

_____

_____

If you don't have any miracles or testimonies to share, I pray God will do the impossible for you so you can share with others. Now you can write your own miracle.

_____

_____

_____

_____

_____

_____

_____

_____

If you don't have any miracles or testimonies to share, I pray God will do the impossible for you so you can share with others. Now you can write your own miracle.

_____

_____

_____

_____

_____

_____

_____

If you don't have any miracles or testimonies to share, I pray God will do the impossible for you so you can share with others. Now you can write your own miracle.

_____

_____

_____

_____

_____

_____

_____

f you don't have any miracles or testimonies to share, I pray God will do the impossible for you so you can share with others. Now you can write your own miracle.

_____

_____

_____

_____

_____

_____

_____

_____

If you don't have any miracles or testimonies to share, I pray God will do the impossible for you so you can share with others. Now you can write your own miracle.

_____

_____

_____

_____

_____

_____

_____

_____

www.ingramcontent.com/pod-product-compliance
Lightning Source LLC
Chambersburg PA
CBHW060119050426
42448CB00010B/1938